DISCAR

D0431732

COMMUNICATION
AROUND THE WORLD

By Jeff Sferazza

Gareth Stevens
PUBLISHING

Please visit our website, www.garethstevens.com. For a free color catalog of all our high-quality books, call toll free 1-800-542-2595 or fax 1-877-542-2596.

Cataloging-in-Publication Data

Names: Sferazza, Jeff.
Title: Communication around the world / Jeff Sferazza.
Description: New York : Gareth Stevens Publishing, 2019. | Series: Adventures in culture | Includes glossary and index.
Identifiers: LCCN ISBN 9781538218570 (pbk.) | ISBN 9781538218556 (library bound) | ISBN 9781538218587 (6 pack)
Subjects: LCSH: Communication–Juvenile literature. | Telecommunication–Juvenile literature.
Classification: LCC P91.2 S44 2019 | DDC 302.2–dc23

Published in 2019 by
Gareth Stevens Publishing
111 East 14th Street, Suite 349
New York, NY 10003

Copyright © 2019 Gareth Stevens Publishing

Designer: Katelyn E. Reynolds
Editor: Meta Manchester

Photo credits: Cover, p. 1 leungchopan/Shutterstock.com; pp. 2–24 (background texture) Flas100/Shutterstock.com; p. 5 Paco Navarro/Blend Images/Getty Images; pp. 7, 11 xPACIFICA/Iconica/Getty Images; p. 9 Ranveig Thattai/Wikipedia.org; p. 13 © Rick Elkins/Moment/Getty Images; p. 15 CommerceandCultureAgency/The Image Bank/Getty Images; p. 17 Mario Tama/Getty Images; p. 19 Jean Chung/Bloomberg via Getty Images; p. 21 Ourania2005/Moment Open/Getty Images.

All rights reserved. No part of this book may be reproduced in any form without permission in writing from the publisher, except by a reviewer.

Printed in the United States of America

CPSIA compliance information: Batch #CS18GS: For further information contact Gareth Stevens, New York, New York at 1-800-542-2595.

CONTENTS

Boldface words appear in the glossary.

All Around the World!

People **communicate** through movement, touch, sound, and writing. Many **cultures** have their own language. People in some cultures learn more than one language to communicate with their neighbors. In fact, half the people on Earth speak more than one language!

5

Spoken Language

There are over 7,000 languages! Half the world speaks only 10 main languages. Mandarin Chinese has the most speakers with around 1.2 billion people! Four countries—India, Nigeria, Indonesia, and Papua New Guinea—are home to one-third of all world languages.

China

好好学习　天天

7

Written Language

Only about half of the world's languages have a writing system. In some countries, such as Greenland and Norway, almost every person is **literate**! But in other countries, such as South Sudan, many people are **illiterate**.

Norway

The largest alphabet is Khmer from Cambodia. It has 74 letters! The shortest alphabet, Rotokas from Papua New Guinea, has only 12 letters. Some languages have **characters**. Chinese characters have strokes that are done in a certain order and direction.

11

Phones

Landlines are phones connected by cables. Before cell phones, many people had landlines in their homes. Pay phones, public landlines you pay to use, were also **popular** before cell phones. Pay phones aren't used as much today, but they're still popular in India.

India

13

Cell Phones

In the United Arab Emirates, almost everyone owns a cell phone. Cell phones are also popular in Africa, where few houses have landlines. People in Kenya sometimes share cell phones.

Kenya

15

Many people around the world own smartphones. People with smartphones use messaging **apps** to communicate. WhatsApp is the most popular messaging app in more than 100 countries, but WeChat is the most popular in China!

Brazil

17

The Internet

Many people communicate over the internet using email. But some places don't have the internet at all! In South Korea, **internet cafés** are popular places to play video games. This is a fun way to meet people and talk to friends.

internet café in South Korea

19

Whistling Languages

In some places, people communicate by **whistling**! Today, only six people know sfyria, a whistled language in Antia, Greece. Before cell phones, messages from Athens, Greece, were called into Antia's only phone, then whistled in sfyria to people up to 2.5 miles (4 km) away!

GLOSSARY

app: a program downloaded onto a smartphone

character: a written or printed symbol

communicate: to share thoughts or feelings by sound, movement, or writing

culture: the beliefs and ways of life of a group of people

illiterate: not able to read or write

internet café: a café where people can pay to go online

literate: able to read and write

popular: liked by many people

whistle: to make a sound by blowing breath through lips or teeth

FOR MORE INFORMATION

BOOKS

Boothroyd, Jennifer. *From Typewriters to Text Messages: How Communication Has Changed.* Minneapolis, MN: Lerner Publications Co., 2012.

Challen, Paul. *Communication in the Ancient World.* New York, NY: Crabtree Publishing Company, 2012.

Kalman, Bobbie. *Communication: Then and Now.* New York, NY: Crabtree Publishing Company, 2014.

WEBSITES

My Grandmother's Lingo
www.sbs.com.au/mygrandmotherslingo
Play this online game to learn Marra, a native Australian language spoken by only three people today!

Chillola
www.chillola.com
Play fun games to learn Spanish, French, German, and Italian words.

Publisher's note to educators and parents: Our editors have carefully reviewed these websites to ensure that they are suitable for students. Many websites change frequently, however, and we cannot guarantee that a site's future contents will continue to meet our high standards of quality and educational value. Be advised that students should be closely supervised whenever they access the internet.

INDEX